LAUGH OUT LOUD!
THE SILLY SAFARI JOKE BOOK

Sean Connolly and Kay Barnham

WINDMILL
BOOKS

New York

Published in 2012 by Windmill Books, LLC
303 Park Avenue South, Suite # 1280, New York, NY 10010-3657

First Edition

Editor: Joe Harris
Illustrations: Adam Clay
Layout Design: Notion Design

Library of Congress Cataloging-in-Publication Data

Connolly, Sean, 1956–
  The silly safari joke book / by Sean Connolly and Kay Barnham. — 1st ed.
       p. cm. — (Laugh out loud!)
  Includes index.
  ISBN 978-1-61533-361-5 (library binding) — ISBN 978-1-61533-399-8 (pbk.) — ISBN 978-1-61533-463-6
  (6-pack)
  1. Animals—Juvenile humor. 2. Safaris—Juvenile humor. I. Barnham, Kay. II. Title.
  PN6231.A5C665 2012
  818'.602—dc22
                                                   2010052149
Printed in the United States of America

For more great fiction and nonfiction, go to www.windmillbooks.com

CPSIA Compliance Information: Batch #AS2011WM: For Further Information contact Windmill Books, New York, New York at 1-866-478-0556
SL001835US

CONTENTS

SILLY SAFARI

What did the blue whale say when he crashed into the bottlenose dolphin?
"I didn't do it on porpoise."

Where do reindeer run around and around in circles?
In Lapland.

What side of a porcupine is the sharpest?
The outside.

What do you call a giraffe with one leg?
Eileen.

Why did the lion
spit out the clown?
Because he tasted
funny.

SILLY SAFARI

What did the tiger eat
after he'd had all his
teeth pulled out?
The dentist.

What do you call a sheep
with no legs?
A cloud.

Why do giraffes
have such long
necks?
Because they
have very smelly
feet.

What do you get if you cross a kangaroo and an elephant?
Very big holes in your lawn.

What do you call someone who lives with a pack
of wolves?
Wolfgang.

SILLY SAFARI

What does an octopus
wear in the winter?
A coat of arms.

What do you call an
elephant in a phone
booth?
Stuck.

Where do
sharks come
from?
Finland.

What's the
difference between a fish and a piano?
You can't tuna fish!

Why do insects hum?
Because they can never remember the words!

What's the best way to catch a fish?
Get someone to throw it at you.

What's black and white and red all over?
A sunburned penguin!

What do you get if you cross a crocodile with a camera?
A snapshot!

Where are elephants found?
They're so huge, it's quite difficult to lose them in the first place.

Why wasn't the girl scared when a shark swam past her?
She'd been told it was a man-eater.

What's an elephant's favorite game?
Squash.

SILLY SAFARI

A police officer saw a man walking down the street with a penguin. He told the man to take the penguin to the zoo. "Good idea," the man said, and off he went.

The next day, the police officer saw the man again. He still had the penguin with him.

"I told you to take that penguin to the zoo," the police officer said.

"I did," the man replied. "He really enjoyed that, so today I'm taking him to the movies."

First leopard: Hey, is that a jogger over there?
Second leopard: Yes, great, I love fast food!

What do you get if you cross a snake with a bird?
A feather boa constrictor!

What's gray, has four legs, and a trunk?
A mouse going on vacation.

SILLY SAFARI

What did the short-sighted porcupine say to the cactus?
"Ah, there you are, dad!"

What do penguins do in their spare time?
They chill.

Spotted in the library:
"I Fell Down a Rabbit Hole" by Alison Wonderland.

What do you call a dead skunk?
Ex-stinked!

Why was the mother firefly sad?
Because her children weren't very bright!

What is the best thing to do when a hippo sneezes?
Get out of the way!

SiLLY SAFARi

What lives in a forest and tells the dullest stories ever heard?
A wild boar!

What did the silliest kid in school call his pet zebra?
"Spot!"

What would you do if a jellyfish stung you?
I'd break every bone in its body!

What does a frog use to put up shelves?
A toad's tool!

How did the fruit bats go into Noah's Ark?
In pears!

SILLY SAFARI

Why are hyenas always falling out?
They always have a bone to pick with each other!

What are the scariest dinosaurs?
Terror dactyls!

What do you call a criminal bird?
An illegal eagle!

What sort of fish would you find in a bird cage?
A perch!

What sort of horses do monsters ride?
Night mares!

SILLY SAFARI

Which animal is the best rapper?
The hip-hop-opotamus!

What is a big game hunter?
Someone who can't find the football stadium!

What is a porcupine's least favorite game?
Leapfrog!

Did you hear about the brown bear who tripped and fell into a blender?
It was a grizzly accident.

Why can you never trick a snake?
Because you can't pull his leg!

Why did cavemen paint pictures of rhinoceroses and hippopotamuses? Because they couldn't spell their names!

Where do penguins vote? At the South Poll.

Why does a cow moo? Because its horns don't work.

Why are snails' shells so shiny? They use snail varnish.

Where do giraffes go to be taught? High school.

Why was the zebra put in charge of the jungle army?
Because he had the most stripes!

How do you catch a squirrel?
Climb a tree and act like a nut.

What's big, furry, and flies?
A hot-air baboon.

How do you stop moles from digging up your lawn?
Hide the shovels.

What's the difference between a crazy rabbit and a counterfeit ten-dollar bill?
One's a mad bunny and the other's bad money.

SiLLY SAFARi

What sea creatures do you find on legal documents?
Seals.

Why should you never trust a whale with your deepest, darkest secrets?
Because they're all blubbermouths.

Where do camels keep their money?
In sand banks.

Where do tadpoles change into frogs?
In a croakroom.

What sort of animal will never oversleep?
A llama clock!

15

SILLY SAFARI

What do rhinoceroses have that no other animal has?
Baby rhinoceroses.

What do you get if you cross an angry sheep with a mad cow?
An animal that's in a baaaaaaaaaaaaaaaad mooooooooooooood.

Why can't leopards hide from hunters?
Because they are always spotted!

When do kangaroos propose marriage?
In leap years!

Where do rabbits learn to fly?
In the Hare Force!

SILLY SAFARI

Did you hear
about the
spiders who got
married?
They had a huge
webbing.

What job did the
spider get?
Web designer!

What do you call
a worm in a fur
coat?
A caterpillar!

What do you call a bad-tempered bee?
A grumblebee.

Doctor, I think I'm a frog.
So what's the problem?
I'm sure I'm going to croak.

What do you get if you cross a dinosaur with a fish?
Jurassic shark!

What do you call a telephone operator for alligators!
A croco-dial!

Did you hear about the wizard who made honey?
He was a spelling bee!

What do you call pigs who write to each other?
Pen pals!

How do elephants travel?
In jumbo jets!

What do camels wear when they play hide-and-seek?
Camel-flage.

What is a porpoise's favorite TV show?
Whale of Fortune.

What do you get if you cross a sheep with a bucket of water?
A wet blanket.

What did the rabbit say when it went bald?
Hare today, gone tomorrow!

Which bird is always out of breath?
A puffin.

SILLY SAFARI

Why do sick crabs walk sideways?
Because their medicine has side-effects!

What do you call a man who delivers Christmas presents to lions and tigers?
Santa Claws!

How do you stop a skunk from smelling?
Hold his nose!

How can you tell if there's an elephant in the fridge?
You can't shut the door!

Why did the elephant refuse to play cards with his two friends?
Because one of them was lion and the other was a cheetah!

What do you call an owl that robs the rich and gives to the poor?
Robin Hoot!

What do toads say when they greet each other?
"Wart's new with you?"

What is a goat's favorite food?
Alpha-butt soup!

What do you get if you cross a leopard and a bunch of flowers?
A beauty spot!

Doctor, I think I'm a crocodile!
Don't worry—you'll soon snap out of it!

How do you get around on
the seabed?
By taxi-crab!

What went into
the lion's cage
at the zoo and
came out
without a
scratch?
Another lion!

Why was the
mother flea
depressed?
All her children had gone to the dogs!

How do you know if there's an elephant in your
refrigerator?
Look for footprints in the cheesecake!

How do you get down from a camel?
You don't. You get down from a goose.

SiLLY SAFARi

How do you stop a rhinoceros from charging?
Take away its cash register.

What happened to the shark that swallowed a bunch of keys?
He got lockjaw!

Which animal was out of bounds?
The exhausted kangaroo.

What do you give a deaf fish?
A herring aid.

What do you call a hippo at the South Pole?
Lost!

SILLY SAFARI

What do you get if you cross a snake with a builder?
A boa constructor.

Where does a blackbird go for a drink?
To a crowbar.

What do porcupines say when they hug?
"Ouch!"

What do you get if you cross a fish with an elephant?
Swimming trunks.

What do you call
a monkey who
is king of the
jungle?
Henry the Ape!

What do you call an
85-year-old ant?
An antique!

What do horses
wear at the
beach?
Clip clops.

Why do rabbits
have fur coats?
Because they'd
look silly in
leather jackets.

Teacher: Billy, what
is a wombat?
Pupil: It's what you
use to play "wom," Miss Adams!

Why did the hyena do so badly at school?
He thought everything was a joke.

Who do fish borrow
money from?
A loan shark.

Knock knock!
Who's there?
Orang.
Orang who?
Orang the
doorbell but no
one answered,
so now I'm
knocking!

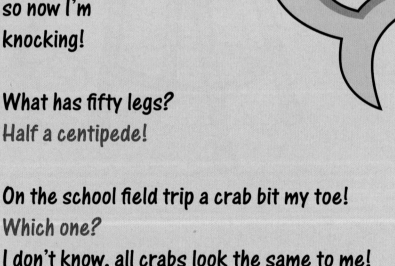

What has fifty legs?
Half a centipede!

On the school field trip a crab bit my toe!
Which one?
I don't know, all crabs look the same to me!

What made the fly fly?
The spider spied her.

What happened when the frog's car broke down?
It was toad away.

What is a sheep's favorite newspaper?
The Wool Street Journal.

Why are fish easy to weigh?
They have their own scales.

What do lizards put on their bathroom walls?
Rep-tiles.

Why are elephants all wrinkly?
Have you ever tried to iron one?

What did the celebrity squirrels sign before they got married?
A pre-nutshell agreement.

Did you hear about the angry pig that lost its voice from oinking too much?
It was disgruntled.

What's brown, furry, and has twelve paws?
The three bears.

What goes dash-dash-squeak, dash-dash-dash-squeak, dot-dot-dash-squeak, dot-dot-dot-squeak, dot-squeak?
Mouse code.

What are the strongest creatures in the ocean?
Mussels.

What is a fish's favorite type of music?
Bubble rap.

What's a carpenter's favorite sea creature?
A hammerhead shark.

Why did Bo Peep lose her sheep?
She had a crook with her.

Doctor, I keep thinking I'm a woodworm.
That must be so boring for you.

Why did the pig cross the road really, really slowly?
Because it was a road hog.

What goes
buzzzzzzzz,
and loves to
nibble cheese?
A mouse-quito!

Why do sharks
live in saltwater?
Pepper makes them
sneeze.

What do you call a
short-sighted
dinosaur?
Doyouthinkhesaurus.

What's black and
white and black and white and black and white?
A penguin rolling down a hill.

What kind of a wig has excellent hearing?
An earwig.

SILLY SAFARI

What do you call a sleeping T. rex?
A dinosnore.

What should you do if you see a blue whale?
Try to cheer him up.

What happened when the elephant went on a crash diet?
He wrecked four trucks, seven cars, and a bus!

What do you call a woodpecker with no beak?
A headbanger!

How do dolphins make a decision?
They flipper coin.

Glossary

counterfeit (KOWN-tuhr-fit) a fake copy of something expensive

earwig (EER-wig) a small insect with a long body and two spikes (called "forceps") at its back end

Jurassic (joo-RA-sik) belonging to a time in the distant past when dinosaurs were alive

porpoise (POR-pus) a small kind of whale with a rounded nose

varnish (VAR-nish) a liquid that dries hard and shiny

wombat (WOM-bat) an Australian animal that looks like a small bear

Further Reading

Chatterton, Martin. *What a Hoot!* New York: Kingfisher, 2005.

Dahl, Michael. *Roaring with Laughter*. Mankato, MN: Picture Window Books, 2004.

Winter, Judy A. *Jokes About Animals*. Mankato, MN: Capstone Press, 2010.

Index

Web Sites

For Web resources related to the subject of this book, go to: www.windmillbooks.com/weblinks and select this book's title.